CONTENTS

SPOT THE CHANGES!

Look carefully at the pairs of pictures to identify the differences between them. As the levels progress, so does the difficulty of the puzzles. You will notice a greater number of changes, and these will be increasingly subtle and more finely detailed. Work your way through the book at your own pace and stimulate your powers of observation as you solve each puzzle. Pictures have been altered in a variety of ways. You might find that a cat has a changed paw, a flower has disappeared, a shadow or reflection has been altered, or a rock has appeared. In some puzzles, the changes are found in the smallest details.

Not all puzzles feature just two images. In other puzzles, you'll have to find a single cat hidden somewhere in the picture. In some, you'll have to pinpoint a single change in one of six photographs! If you're stumped, you can find the answers in the back of the book. So, curl up like a cat in your favorite chair, grab a pencil, and start puzzling.

BRAIN GAMES®

PICTURE PUZZLES

CATS

Publications International, Ltd.

ISBN: 978-1-64558-759-0

Manufactured in China.

8 7 6 5 4 3 2 1

Let's get social!
@Publications_International
@PublicationsInternational
@BrainGames.TM
www.pilbooks.com

Answers on page 141.

Answers on page 141.

Answers on page 141.

Answers on page 141.

1.

2.

3.

4.

5.

6.

Answer on page 141.

Answer on page 141.

Answers on page 142.

LEVEL 1   4 CHANGES

Answers on page 142.

1.

2.

3.

4.

5.

6.

Answer on page 142.

Answers on page 142.

Answers on page 143.

Answers on page 143.

Answer on page 143.

Answers on page 143.

1.

2.

3.

4.

5.

6.

Answer on page 143.

Answers on page 143.

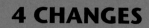

Answers on page 144.

1.

2.

3.

4.

5.

6.

30

Answer on page 144.

FIND THE CAT

Answer on page 144.

Answers on page 145.

FIND THE CAT

Answer on page 145.

Answers on page 145.

Answers on page 145.

Answers on page 145.

Answers on page 146.

44

Answers on page 146.

1.

2.

3.

4.

5.

6.

Answer on page 146.

Answers on page 146.

48

Answers on page 146.

Answers on page 147.

Answers on page 147.

Answers on page 147.

Answers on page 147.

1.

2.

3.

4.

5.

6.

Answer on page 147.

Answers on page 147.

Answers on page 148.

Answers on page 148.

Answers on page 148.

Answers on page 148.

Answers on page 148.

Answers on page 148.

Answers on page 149.

1.

2.

3.

4.

5.

6.

Answer on page 149.

Answers on page 149.

1.

2.

3.

4.

5.

6.

Answer on page 149.

Answers on page 149.

Answers on page 150.

Answers on page 150.

Answer on page 150.

Answers on page 150.

Answers on page 150.

1.

2.

3.

4.

5.

6.

Answer on page 151.

Answers on page 151.

Answers on page 151.

Answers on page 151.

82

Answers on page 151.

1.

2.

3.

4.

5.

6.

Answer on page 151.

83

Answers on page 152.

Answers on page 152.

Answers on page 152.

WHAT'S THE DIFFERENCE?

1.

2.

3.

4.

5.

6.

Answer on page 152.

Answers on page 152.

Answers on page 153.

Answers on page 153.

Answers on page 153.

Answers on page 153.

Answers on page 153.

Answers on page 154.

Answers on page 154.

Answers on page 154.

Answers on page 154.

Answers on page 154.

1.

2.

3.

4.

5.

6.

Answer on page 154.

Answer on page 155.

Answers on page 155.

LEVEL 4   10 CHANGES

Answers on page 155.

Answers on page 155.

Answers on page 155.

111

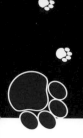

1.

2.

3.

4.

5.

6.

Answer on page 155.

Answers on page 156.

Answers on page 156.

Answers on page 156.

Answers on page 156.

Answers on page 156.

1.

2.

3.

4.

5.

6.

Answer on page 156.

Answers on page 157.

Answers on page 157.

Answers on page 157.

1.

2.

3.

4.

5.

6.

Answer on page 157.

Answers on page 157.

Answers on page 158.

Answers on page 158.

Answers on page 158.

Answers on page 158.

1.

2.

3.

4.

5.

6.

132

Answer on page 158.

Answers on page 158.

Answers on page 159.

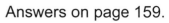

Answers on page 159.

Answers on page 159.

Answers on page 160.

Answers on page 160.

ANSWERS

Page 5

Pages 8-9

Page 6

Page 10

Page 7

Page 11

ANSWERS

Page 12

Page 16

Page 13

Page 17

Pages 14-15

Page 18

ANSWERS

Page 19

Page 23

Pages 20-21

Page 24

Page 22

Page 25

ANSWERS

Pages 26-27

Page 30

Page 28

Page 31

Page 29

Pages 32-33

ANSWERS

Pages 34-35

Pages 38-39

Page 36

Page 40

Page 37

Page 41

ANSWERS

Page 42-43

Page 46

Page 44

Page 47

Page 45

Page 48

ANSWERS

Page 49

Page 53

Pages 50-51

Page 54

Page 52

Page 55

ANSWERS

Page 56

Page 60

Page 57

Page 61

Pages 58-59

Page 62

ANSWERS

Page 63

Pages 66-67

Page 64

Page 68

Page 65

Page 69

ANSWERS

Page 70

Page 74

Page 71

Page 75

Pages 72-73

Page 76

ANSWERS

Page 77

Page 81

Pages 78-79

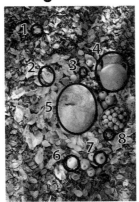

Page 82

Page 80

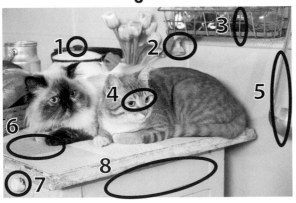

Page 83

ANSWERS

Pages 84-85

Page 88

Page 86

Page 89

Page 87

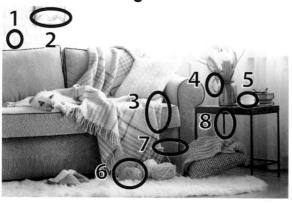

Page 90-91

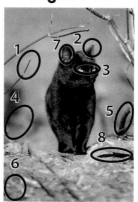

ANSWERS

Page 92

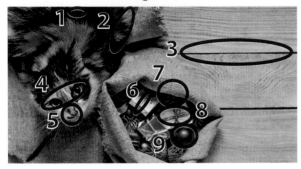

Page 95

Page 93

Pages 96-97

Page 94

Page 98

ANSWERS

Page 99

Pages 102-103

Page 100

Page 104

Page 101

Page 105

ANSWERS

Page 106

Page 109

Page 107

Pages 110-111

Page 108

Page 112

ANSWERS

Page 113

Pages 116-117

Page 114

Page 118

Page 115

Page 119

ANSWERS

Page 120

Page 124

Page 121

Page 125

Pages 122-123

Page 126

ANSWERS

Page 127

Page 131

Pages 128-129

Page 132

Page 130

Page 133

ANSWERS

Page 134

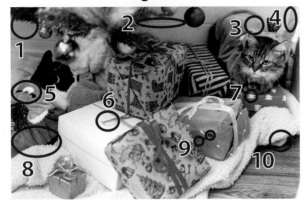

Page 135

Pages 136-137

ANSWERS

Pages 138-139

Page 140